W9-AUM-634

Table Of Contents

CHECK OUT MORE TITLES FROM OUR QUICKLETS SERIES!

Quicklet on Popular Science November 2011

$2.99

BUY NOW

Quicklet – The 7 Habits of Highly Effective People by Stephen Covey

$2.99

BUY NOW

Quicklet on Animal Farm by George Orwell

$2.99

BUY NOW

About The Publisher

Hyperink is the easiest way for anyone to publish a beautiful, high-quality book.

We work closely with subject matter experts to create each book. We cover topics ranging from higher education to job recruiting, from Android apps marketing to barefoot running.

If you have interesting knowledge that people are willing to pay for, especially if you've already produced content on the topic, please reach out to us! There's no writing required and it's a unique opportunity to build your own brand and earn royalties.

Hyperink is based in SF and actively hiring people who want to shape publishing's future. Email us if you'd like to meet our team!

About The Author

The Quicklet Team is dedicated to providing high quality summaries of great books, allowing busy people to learn the most important information from a book in a single sitting.

Quicklet On The World Is Flat

Introduction

About Thomas Friedman

Thomas Friedman is an author, essayist, and columnist. He graduated from University of Minnesota in 1975 with a Bachelor's degree in Mediterranean studies. He obtained his Masters in modern Middle Eastern studies from Oxford in 1978.

Beginning in 1981, Friedman worked for The New York Times covering Middle Eastern stories and conflicts. He then was the Times' Chief White House Correspondent in 1992. Friedman wrote books, and he also made documentaries for the Discovery Channel.

Among his numerous awards are three Pulitzer Prizes, two for international reporting and one for distinguished commentary. He has two other books, *The Lexus and the Olive Tree: Understand Globalization* and *Hot, Flat, and Crowded: Why We Need a Green Revolution — and How It Can Renew America*. Friedman also has a collection of articles published under the title Longitudes and Latitudes: Exploring the World After September 11.

The Significance of The World is Flat

Friedman's book highlights the convergence of the world's technologies, allowing each country a chance to become a leading world power. Friedman calls this phenomenon "flattening" as new information and equipment levels the economic playing field.

The growing relationship between companies, countries, and individuals is a part of the new globalization era, and the world grows smaller and flatter every day. The release of new technology gives individuals powerful connectivity to others, resulting in the convergence and collaboration of great ideas.

Friedman created an intelligent book with the keen eye and astuteness of an economist. However, his exploration of globalization, economics, and technology is tempered with the natural story-telling abilities of an award-winning journalist.

Forgot Your Christmas Shopping? Gift A Copy Of This Quicklet To 3 Friends!

Happy holidays!

To ring in 2012, we're offering a special bonus to Hyperink customers who purchase special titles.

For the first 500 customers only, if you click on this link, you can send up to 3 bonus copies of the **Quicklet on The World Is Flat** to your friends and family!

Here's the full link: https://hyperink.wufoo.com/forms/quicklet-on-the-world-is-flat/

In the following 1-minute form, simply fill out your email, and the emails of *up to 3 people* that you'd like to receive your gift.

Within 24 hours, they'll receive a unique download link for a free copy of the **Quicklet on The World Is Flat**.

We take your privacy very seriously, and we promise that we will NEVER spam you or share your email with any 3rd parties.

Please email hello@hyperink.com if you have any questions or feedback.

Thanks and happy 2012! This bonus is only for the first 500 customers, so get on it!

-The Hyperink Team

Facebook: www.facebook.com/hyperink
Twitter: www.twitter.com/hyperink

List Of Important People

Thomas Friedman: Thomas Friedman is the author and narrative voice of The World is Flat. Friedman explores the globe and speaks with hundreds of leaders in the technological and economic fields to find out exactly how the world is flattening. He uses anecdotes to explain each of his points.

Christopher Columbus: Christopher Columbus is the Spanish voyager and who discovered the Americas purely by accident. On his way to India, he took a western route rather than sailing around Africa. According to Friedman, his discovery ushered in the age of Globalization 1.0. His breakthrough caused the world to grow smaller and different people groups to be connected.

Jim Barksdale: Jim Barksdale is the former Netscape CEO, the man responsible for Friedman's Flattener #2: When Netscape Went Public. The company provided a consistent web-browser experience for everyone on any computer. Barksdale and the rest of the Netscape staff wanted every person to use the world wide web as a tool for connectivity.

Willy Loman: Willy Loman is the main character of Arthur Miller's play Death of a Salesman. Loman tragically believed in the promise of the American Dream, but didn't understand that hard work provided happiness and results. The character also believed that being well-liked would bring him success. According to Friedman, these ideas are not present in a flat world; because people are trying to cut corners and costs, individual personalities are often disregarded as unimportant. Friedman refers to Loman multiple times in the book.

Bill Gates: Bill Gates is the President and CEO of Microsoft. According the Friedman, his vision helped bring about the flattening. However, Friedman gives both sides of his business strategy. He explains that Gates and Microsoft have been leveling the playing field, but his exclusive and cut-throat tactics are also discussed. Friedman refers to Gates as well as Microsoft multiple times in the book.

Osama bin Laden: Osama bin Laden was the founder and leader of the terrorist organization al-Qaeda. As well as numerous other rebellious attacks, his organization was responsible for the September 11 attacks on America. Friedman uses bin Laden as an example of connectivity and global flattening when it is used as in a negative and combative way.

Key Terms And Definitions

Flattening: The way the world's technology impacts the globe which interconnects all individuals laterally; everyone is on a level playing field because they can contact anyone. Information is at their fingertips. Commerce is much easier because the global market is connected to individuals.

Globalization 1.0: The period of time from 1492-1800; ushered in by Columbus' discovery of America, the world was connected by governments and religions. The main force behind Globalization 1.0 is that countries and religions wanted to control the biggest section of the world in order to have the best resources available.

Globalization 2.0: The period of time from 1800-2000; multinational companies were connecting the world. The Industrial Revolution led this change, along with the English's and Dutch's efforts to place their companies in multiple countries.

Globalization 3.0: The period from 2000 on; individuals competed globally amongst each other as well as companies. While there are certain barriers due to governmental control over physical boundaries, the person-to-person connectivity is still present.

Homesourcing: When a company allows people to work from their own home rather than come into an office.

Ten Forces that Flattened the World

These ten events, innovations, and companies in the late 20th century and on played a significant role in flattening the world:

1. Fall of the Berlin Wall
2. When Netscape Went Public
3. Interconnectivity of Computers and Web-Based Applications
4. Open-Source Movement
5. Outsourcing to India for Y2K
6. Offshoring to China
7. Walmart and Supply Chains
8. UPS and Insourcing

9. Google and Informing
10. Mobile Access

Triple Convergence: The period of Globalization 3.0 when companies from all over the world began to work together and create new technologies for doing business.

Zippie: A young person from a formerly-closed country who now thrives in a flattened world.

The Great Sorting Out: When business have to connect and collaborate horizontally (with other businesses) rather than command and control vertically (within their own business).

Free Trade: An economic theory which suggests that each nation should focus on its best, most advantageous products and have an open trading policy with other countries doing the same. The result is an overall gain in trade and income levels.

Untouchables: Friedman's name for the jobs that Americans need to prepare for. In a flat economy, these are the jobs that will never be outsourced.

The Quiet Crisis: Describing the state of America and its future. The crisis is not immediate, but rather imminent, if America does not try to compete in a global economy by bettering education. There are three "dirty secrets" of America that put the country at a disadvantage:

1. The numbers gap
2. The ambition gap
3. The education gap

Glocalization: The ability of a culture to absorb and merge foreign ideas with its own practices in order to get ahead.

Summary Of Chapter One: While I Was Sleeping

"This flattening process is happening at warp speed and directly or indirectly touching a lot more people on the planet at once" (49).

Friedman begins his book with a chapter describing the how he came to realize that the world was, in fact, "flat." He travelled all over the formerly-closed countries (India, China, and Japan) to look at the ways they have integrated themselves into America's base infrastructure.

Many of the services and products America receives are outsourced. The telephone help desk has become a booming business for India, as many of its workers receive high pay, benefits, and incentives. Manufacturing plants in China build parts for America.

The lost cost of labor allows American companies to place a smaller price tag on the finished product. This in turn will help lower the inflation which accumulated during the years of an economically non-flat world. However, the immediate downside is that Americans are loosing their jobs. What starts out as a business' well-intentioned move makes life difficult for individuals.

Friedman explains that the military has taken to the new technology and turned their hierarchical system and made it flatter. As Friedman explored a base in Iraq, he watched the live feed from around Iraq taken by Predator drone. This drone was actually being "flown" remotely by an expert in Las Vegas, Nevada. Central Command in Tampa, regional headquarters and Qatar, the Pentagon, and the CIA were all able to watch the same live feed.

Some companies are choosing to combat the move to other countries by doing what is called homesourcing. The workers are happier when working from their own home. Thus, their work load and productivity increases merely because they can work in a comfortable environment.

The people of these countries have taken the smallest jobs and turned them into full-fledged businesses. These businesses have brought the countries to the forefront of global economics, leading Friedman to begin his thought process on how the world became flat.

Summary Of Chapter Two: The Ten Forces That Flattened The World

"The Bible tells us that God created the world in six days and on the seventh day he rested. Flattening the world took a little longer" (50).

Friedman finds himself recalling the ten events which flattened the world:

Fall of the Berlin Wall: Before this point, communism and other oppressive governments kept their countries from joining the world. When the Wall fell, the people of these countries were able to contribute to the global dynamic.

When Netscape Went Public: Netscape, the internet browser company, changed the way the internet worked. It allowed for people of all ages to browse internet pages and sites by allowing for open communication between developers. Their efforts were directly propelled by the idea that Microsoft, the company monopolizing the internet market, wouldn't be able to dominate the internet completely.

Interconnectivity of Computers and Web-Based Applications: The computers and different web applications were able to inter-connect with each other. Before this point, people were limited to only connecting if they had the same web browser. For example, a person with a Netscape browser couldn't interact with a person using Internet Explorer. Even in a business, every department had to work with the same internet software. When different companies started merging their internet software with others, people had a level of connectivity never before possible.

Open-Source Movement: From different types of uploading, from internet applications to information, people have wanted to participate and contribute to the world's conversation. The internet is the perfect place for them to allow their voice to be heard. Because many technical engineers only want to further the technology, many teamed up and allowed for free use and improvement on their ideas. This freedom allowed many people to work on the technology, thus advancing the ideas and applications. The most popular user-driven open-source content provider is Wikipedia, which allows anyone to modify or edit their encyclopedia of knowledge. Even though the changes are moderated, the website is still a unique force in the internet community.

Outsourcing to India for Y2K: Y2K was the first time that India was able to become a force in the technological world. The workers in India could reach American computers and reset the computers' internal clocks to the right date so they would not crash. It was cost-efficient, and it gave India a chance to show that they were eager to become a leader in the world economy. Ever since Y2K, businesses realize that outsourcing their basic functions is a smart move financially. The outsourced employees are smart and efficient, and they work for less than Americans due to lower costs of living.

Offshoring to China: Much like outsourcing for India, China became a manufacturing hub once the country lifted its strict regulations on trading. Companies could make the same quality products for much less because the economy in China isn't as inflated as in America. It was difficult to get the workers and manufacturers to understand the concept of exceeding quotas. However, the work started flowing smoothly once Chinese managers realized that more products meant more money.

Walmart and Supply Chains: Walmart is the prime example of a supply chain, a company which hosts multitudes of items for very little cost to the consumer. Supply chains cut out the middle man and deal directly with the manufacturer. Even using its own delivery trucks shrinks the product cost down by a significant amount. This process, along with other shortcuts, ensures the lowest prices and beats competing stores.

UPS and Insourcing: UPS is a leader of insourcing, where the company will hire its own workers to work in factories of manufacturers in order to ensure the swiftest delivery. Friedman explains that UPS hires employees to work as liaisons for the companies that hire them for delivery. UPS has people working in computer repairs and shoe selection, among hundreds of other capacities.

Google and Informing: Everybody with internet access has the ability to find out any information with a few clicks of a button. Because of search engines, people are more informed than any previous generation and people have become self-empowered. There is no longer a need for direct contact with field experts because their ideas can be found in a few mere seconds.

Mobile Access: Personal mobile devices allow the freedom to have the world at your fingertips on a single device. The Digital Age has revolutionized with its ability to have connectivity at any point in the world. Although there have been cell phones and other mobile devices, the integration of the internet and other applications has allowed for all kinds of actions. From downloading to file-swapping, there is nothing a user cannot do at any second of the day.

Summary Of Chapter Three: The Triple Convergence

"Thanks to the triple convergence, this new flat-world platform is, in effect, blowing away our walls, ceilings, and floors — all at the same time" (232).

Friedman knows that each of the ten forces in the previous chapter could not have flattened the world on their own. He suggests that triple convergence was the only way that these ideas could have been spread so rapidly.

Convergence 1: The ten flatteners spread across the world in small bits. Only major companies were at the forefront of the ten flatteners, and only they saw the potential of the new technologies.

Convergence 2: The users need to use new technologies in order for the new ways of business to spread. The companies began to collaborate with each other, allowing for a greater number of technologies to spread.

Convergence 3: The countries of the world get their hands on new technology, and they combine their own technology with the pieces they acquired.

Because the world is flattening, Friedman realizes that talent is beginning to matter more than geographic location. For instance, young adults from China are finally starting to become successful. They have the same opportunities as Western young adults to work for powerful companies in America and Europe.

Summary Of Chapter Four: The Great Sorting Out

"The flattening process relentlessly trims the fat out of business and life, but … fat is what gives life taste and texture. Fat is also what keeps us warm" (257).

Because the world has been flattened, Friedman believes that companies need to adapt to the new playing field instead of fighting it. He suggests that the companies expand horizontally (to connect and collaborate) rather than expand vertically (to focus on their own business).

He also suggests that individuals will lose their identities as the lines between consumer and employee, taxpayer and shareholder begin to blur.

Friedman uses an example of a company in Indiana outsourcing jobs to India in order to save money. He asks if outsourcing to India was taking advantage of cheap labor, even if it meant that the outsourcing created jobs for thousands of Indians.

Regardless, Friedman knows that the high speed that people connect has allowed for people to forget the personality and humanity at the other end of the phone or computer screen. Everyone wants the lowest prices, but they forget that low prices come at the expense of people's job benefits and health insurance. Values and morality are at stake, unfortunately, and Friedman can only attribute their possible demise to the flattened world.

Summary Of Chapter Five: America And Free Trade

"There may be a limit to the number of good factory jobs in the world, but there is no limit to the number of idea-generated jobs in the world" (267).

Free trade laws are a double-edged sword for Friedman. On one hand, Americans will certainly lose jobs to outsourcing. However, Friedman believes that closing borders to trade will eventually hinder a country from becoming a superpower in the ever-flattening global economy.

According to Friedman, free trade laws allow a company's consumer base to expand by the thousands.

While cutting stateside jobs is a downside, the growth of industries and consumerism will allow companies to expand, thus hiring more employees. Friedman believes that the only way to win internationally is to cultivate and empower the brightest minds all around the globe. At the moment, Americans only compete with other Americans for jobs. But this all changes in a global economy.

Summary Of Chapter Six: The Untouchables

"There is no sugar-coating the new challenge: Every young American today would be wise to think of himself or herself as competing against every young Chinese, Indian, or Brazilian" (276).

Because many American jobs will be outsourced in the future, Friedman believes that people should prepare themselves by choosing career paths that cannot be moved to another country. There are many different types of Untouchables according to Friedman:

1. **Collaborator** and orchestrator: mediates between businesses as well as between different departments in the same business.
2. **Synthesizer:** creates new ideas and products by merging two different ideas or products.
3. **Explainer:** explains complex ideas with ease and simplicity to those who are not in a certain field.
4. **Leverager:** locates problems and fixes them quickly.
5. **Adapter:** a worker who does not specialize, but instead can learn all types of jobs quickly and efficiently; the adaptable worker can thrive in any circumstance.
6. **Personalizer:** performs jobs that cannot be outsourced, like waiting tables or cutting hair.
7. **Localizer:** understands global economics and can tailor a business to bring the same ideas to a single community

According to Friedman, this list is essentially a "help wanted" ad. These jobs will always be important, and necessary, in a flattened global economy.

Summary Of Chapter Seven: The Quiet Crisis

"The U.S. today is in a truly global environment, and those competitor countries are not only wide awake, they are running a marathon while we are running sprints" (326).

According to Friedman, America has three "dirty little secrets" which haunt the American education system. In order to excel in the global economy, he believes that we need to fix them immediately.

1. The Numbers Gap: The number of engineers in America is dwindling from the 1950's. Now, the majority of science-driven students is found in China. 60% of the students are working toward an engineering degree.
2. The Ambition Gap: Company heads know that using outsourced labor for their lower-paying jobs will give them increased productivity. In particular, Indian workers will take a call operating job and perform it with more enthusiasm than most American workers in the same position.
3. The Education Gap: The young people in other countries are pushing themselves harder in sciences and engineering than in America. This allows them to have an extremely competitive edge in American companies over less-experienced American workers.

Americans are at a place of misunderstanding if they believe that countries like China, India, and Japan only want to work for America and create its technology. In fact, they want to exceed and dominate our economy, putting them in the #1 economical spot on the globe.

Summary Of Chapter Eight: This Is Not A Test

"The main challenge to America today comes from the fact that all the walls are being taken down, and other countries can now compete with us much more directly" (361).

Comparing the global economic situation with that of the Cold War crisis, Americans don't see an immediate threat when they look at the current state of the world. Friedman believes that Americans will need to work hard at preparing workers and young people for the new, flattened future by training them well and allowing for creativity in the workplace.

One reason Friedman believes that America is behind is because our politicians know nothing about economics or technology. Compared to China and Japan, where the politicians are scientists and engineers, the leaders of America can never hope to truly understand this new flattened world.

Another cause of America's lag is that its workers are conditioned to do one type of job for a lifetime. According to Friedman, companies should be focusing on giving Americans the tools to better educate and adapt themselves for what changes the future holds.

While the companies might lose more workers in the short term, this will cause a long-term attraction for job seekers to their companies. Also, this education will help Americans meet the future with a determination

Losing jobs is inevitable in a flat economy. However, America should still allow for its laid-off workers to receive wage insurance. This is a policy which compensates workers who have to switch industries due to a lay-off. Until they can learn enough about the trade to make a decent wage, the government would compensate them for a few years if they met certain criteria.

Summary Of Chapter Nine: The Virgin Of Guadalupe

"As the world goes flat, and the more and more of the tools of collaboration get distributed and commoditized, the gap between cultures that have the will, the way, and the focus to quickly adopt these new tools and apply them and those that do not will matter more" (410).

Friedman opens with an example of how the miniature statues of the Virgin of Guadalupe, the patron saint of Mexico, is being imported into Mexico by China. He states that this is a serious matter for Mexico, whose only contribution to the global market is its low-wage manufacturing plants. Now, importing small pieces of plastic is cheaper than making it themselves.

This is a terrifying aspect for economically developing countries. If they cannot afford to manufacture their own goods, they will soon be out of business. While this low-wage competition is good for powerhouses like America, developing countries won't be able to sustain themselves if they lose to a country that can offer a cheaper services.

In order for developing countries to succeed, Friedman believes that the leaders and strategists should allow their entrepreneurs the ability to succeed in a flat world. Countries that will not adapt to the changing global economy will be crushed by their own decisions. However, developing countries that embrace the new flat world will do well because they were willing to modify their own economy for the future of their country.

Friedman looks to Ireland as an example of a country that has benefited from the flattened global economy. Its government started focusing on providing higher education opportunities as well as support for businesses. Now, nine out of ten of the world's top pharmaceutical companies have operations in Ireland, and other industries have started looking to Ireland as a home for their companies.

To make his point, Friedman cites that the countries that have thrived in a flattened economy have cultures that glocalize. Mixing "globalization" and "localization," a culture which learns from the successful practices of economically larger countries. In turn, this culture applies those practices to its own. Soon, it reaps the benefits. Because these countries believe that adaptability is the key to survival, they have thrived. Conversely, countries that repel other cultures are economically weak.

Summary Of Chapter Ten: How Companies Cope

"If you want to flourish in the flattening world, you better understand that whatever can be done will be done — and much faster than you think. The only question is whether it will be done by you or to you"
(426).

In the same vein as countries and glocalization, the companies that can best adapt to the new global economy will be the ones to withstand the flattening.

Creativity and adaptability is key, and companies need to realize what positions are immediately important for the customers' satisfaction and outsource the rest in order to cut back on spending.

Outsourcing then will be a form of company growth; it will allow the company to invest more money to better serve its customers.

Summary Of Chapter Eleven: The Unflat World

"There is absolutely no guarantee that everyone will use these new technologies, or the triple convergence, for the benefit of themselves, their countries, or humanity" (460).

While the world is flattening at a face pace, Friedman makes mention that the world is not flat yet. From students using technology to cheat on test to al-Qaeda using the internet as a means of terrorism distribution, there are still major setbacks that can negatively affect certain people groups or parts of the world should the global market continue to flatten.

Friedman also realizes that there is a threat to the earth's natural resources as people deplete the earth in order to compete with other countries and companies. If every person in every countries strives to have the biggest and the best, the drain on resources will be devastating.

Summary Of Chapter Twelve: The Dell Theory Of Conflict Prevention

"As the world flattens, one of the most interesting dramas to watch in international relations will be the interplay between the traditional global threats and the newly emergent global supply chains" (521).

While some areas of the world oppose global flattening, Friedman believes that it can be a good thing for company-to-company as well as country-to-country relations. The joint venture of two companies ensures that they will not go to war, but instead that they will continue to work together for the greater good of their unified product.

Friedman uses Dell as an example. The computer company uses parts from different countries in order to seamlessly create the best product available. At the same time, each of these countries works together in order to build components that function together.

By working together, the countries' efforts and goals become unified. If one country went to war with another, their relationships with Dell would be ruined, and they would lose a great deal of their economic income. Now, when countries have political conflicts, they have to weight whether or not the political conflict outweighs their economic interests.

On the other side of the matter, open communication lines have led to a rise in the joining of negative forces. Al-Qaeda, anarchists, and other terroristic groups have found a medium which allows for them to spread their ideas and, unfortunately, their terror campaigns.

Summary Of Chapter Thirteen: 11/9 Versus 9/11

"In the end, technology alone cannot keep us safe. We really do have to find ways to affect the imagination of those who would use the tools of collaboration to destroy the world that has invented these tools" (549).

The date 11/9 is the date that begins the process of flattening: the fall of the Berlin Wall. While this date is one of creativity and life, 9/11 is just the opposite. The terrorist attack on America saw that the flattening of the world allowed bin Laden to plan his assault.

Even when there were other superpowers threatening the freedom of the world, there was never one as educated in the world's workings as bin Laden. Because of the internet, he had accessed to all the information he needed to concoct his terrorism plan.

However, Friedman warns that this should not be a deterrent for global flattening. With so much positive change happening, it is up to us as a unified world to decide where the new technology and economy can take us.

Like What You're Reading? Spread The Word!

We're a small startup, so we rely on happy readers to help us grow (hopefully, that means you!).

Here are some specific ways you can contribute:

1. Share your success with us! Tell us how the book has helped you
2. Visit our website: and comment on your favorite article
3. Ask our experts a question! We'll answer the best ones directly on the site
4. Send us your feedback or ideas at feedback@hyperink.com!

To make it worth your time (and to thank you for bugging your friends/family), email us after you've done any of the above and we'll give you a **special bonus** as thanks. Trust us, it's worth it!

Thanks!

CHECK OUT MORE TITLES FROM OUR QUICKLETS SERIES!

Quicklet on The Year of Magical Thinking by Joan Didion

$2.99

BUY NOW

Quicklet – Inception

$2.99

BUY NOW

Quicklet On A New Earth

$2.99

BUY NOW